A-Z for Me!

Life Skills for Kids

written by Mitzi Adams

illustrated by Lindsey Jaeger

Copyright © 2020 by Mitzi Adams Studio, LLC
All rights reserved.
No part of this book may be used or reproduced in any manner whatsoever
without written permission except in the case of
brief quotations embodied in critical articles and reviews, and except for enumerated pages 30 and 31,
which may be copied for personal or educational non-commercial use.
The illustrations were made with Micron® pens and Daniel Smith® watercolors on Canson XL Series Mix Media Paper®.
The illustrations, layout, and cover design are by Lindsey Jaeger.

DEDICATION

FOR EVERY CHILD: "Believe in Yourself. Be Brave, Be Courageous, and Never Give Up!"

M.A.: to Dan, Abby, Barret, & Braden…My Everything!

L.J.: to Steve, Lily, and Iris

A **is for ACCEPTANCE**. Accepting others begins with accepting yourself. You are wonderful by just being you! Like snowflakes in winter, no snowflake or person is exactly the same. We may not look the same, but we are ALL humans with unique talents, strengths, and challenges. Loving your unique self grows into accepting others. Look into a mirror and say these words, "I **ACCEPT** MYSELF. I LOVE MYSELF. I AM WONDERFUL. I AM ME!" What makes YOU wonderful?

B is for BELONGING. We all want to be part of a group and belong. Belonging makes you feel happy, safe, included, and accepted. Belonging is a human need, just like food and shelter. Your school, friends, family, church, clubs, and teams are communities that you belong to. Cooperation with others creates friendships, encourages fairness, and acceptance of ALL. Every person has a place in the world and a voice to be heard. YOU MATTER! How will YOU include someone so they **belong**?

C **is for COURAGE**. Courage means doing something even if you feel afraid. It can be trying a new food, speaking up for something you believe in, singing a solo, or trying out for a team. Feeling afraid is part of being courageous and brave. Challenge yourself even if it feels scary—EVERYONE is afraid sometimes! Trying something new may not turn out the way you hoped and that's OK. You learned from your experience. Believe in yourself. Be brave, be **courageous**, and never give up! When have YOU had courage?

D **is for DETERMINATION.** Being determined means having a goal and working hard to meet your goal. Learning to swim, play an instrument, or hitting a homerun takes determination. Your success will not happen overnight. Determination is patience, persistence, and positive thinking. It means you try AGAIN, AGAIN, and AGAIN! Failing happens. You may feel disappointed, frustrated, and afraid to keep trying. Write down your goals and imagine yourself succeeding. What does it feel like when you visualize your success? Be **determined** and all your hard work will pay off! When have YOU shown determination?

E is for **EMPATHY**. Empathy is the ability to understand the feelings of another person. Understanding the feelings of someone else means asking how would you feel if you were in the same situation? Have you ever felt sad when your friend was sad? Have you ever felt happy when they were happy? Connections to people are made through treating them with kindness, respect, and showing empathy. By listening to someone, you are offering reassurance, comfort, and a chance to share their feelings. How have YOU shown **empathy** to someone?

F **is for FRIENDSHIP**. Friendships are important. Playing alone is no fun! Sharing, trusting, laughing, encouraging, giving, and receiving all happen in friendships. A true friend walks with you in good times and when you struggle. If your friend says something hurtful, tell them how you feel. Talking about it is better than staying mad. Sometimes you have to say, "I'm sorry, will you forgive me?" Forgiveness allows you to remain friends. Making new friends and keeping old ones will fill you with joy! What fun things do YOU like to do when YOU are with a **friend**?

G is for **GRATITUDE**. Gratitude means being thankful for what you have. Show gratitude by saying "Thank You". Make a card for someone special. Volunteer to help others. Be positive and show appreciation for all the good things. What is on your Gratitude List: family, friends, your home, food, or your pets? Every day, you get to wake up and make a choice to be grateful. Positivity and gratitude will make you shine! What are some ways YOU show **gratitude**?

H **is for HEALTH**. Treat your body well, it's the only one you have. Eat healthy, go outside, and MOVE your body! Play, run, and ride your bike. Did you know your body is made of mostly water? Water is in your heart, brain, lungs, muscles, and even your skin and bones-so stay hydrated! Sleep restores your energy, improves learning, behavior, memory, and your immune system. WOW, all that from sleep! A clean, healthy body makes for a happy, healthy mind. If you feel upset or anxious, don't bottle up your feelings. You're not alone! Write your feelings in a journal or talk about how you feel with a trusted adult or friend. What do YOU do to stay **healthy**?

I **is for INTEGRITY**. Do YOU do the right thing even when no one is watching? Integrity means keeping your promises, being honest, and treating people fairly. Dishonesty, cheating, stealing, and bullying are wrong. If you make a mistake, be courageous, accept responsibility and apologize. Never do something that dishonors your reputation. Make good choices. Be an example to others and encourage your friends to do what is right. What are ways that YOU have shown **integrity**?

J **is for JOY**. Joy is the happy feeling you get when you help others, feel hopeful, or have a good experience. Joy is found in your daily moments, BIG and small. Admiring a rainbow, watching a peaceful snow fall, and snuggling with your pet are small acts that bring joy. Getting straight A's, making the basketball team, or winning the spelling bee are B-I-G joyful moments. Doing acts of kindness will make your inner light shine and fill you with joy! What makes YOU feel **joyful**?

K **is for KINDNESS.** Kindness is the quality of being friendly, generous, and considerate to others. Eating lunch with a new student, giving a compliment, raking leaves for your neighbor, or donating toys are ways you can show kindness. Being kind connects you to people and makes everyone feel good. Share your beautiful smile and remember that kindness begins with you! How do YOU show **kindness** to others?

L is for **LAUGHTER**. Humor and Joy bring laughter & laughter makes you feel HAPPY! Did you know that laughing is good for your body? Laughter relieves stress and helps you stay healthy. Laughing helps oxygen flow to your heart and brain. Your mood will brighten instantly. Don't take yourself too seriously. Laugh about your embarrassing moments—we've all had them! Connect with friends to tell a funny joke and enjoy the positive feelings. After all, laughter is contagious! How has **laughter** made YOU feel better?

M is for **MANNERS**. Polite manners leave a positive impression. Do you say "Please", "Thank You", and "Excuse Me" to others? When meeting someone new, a handshake, smile, and eye contact are a must. Greetings begin with a "Good Morning" and "Goodbye" is said upon leaving. Respectfully open and hold doors for others. Be quiet in places like libraries, movies, and museums-indoor voices please. Table manners matter! Talking with food in your mouth is just gross. A napkin in your lap helps with spills and embarrassing food-on-your-face moments—OOPS! Using good manners reflects upon you. How do people react when YOU use **good manners**?

N **is for NO!** Saying "NO" to something that doesn't feel right is one of the bravest actions you can do. If you are in a situation where you feel uncomfortable, say "NO", LEAVE, and tell a trusted adult. Speak up for yourself. Say "STOP" if someone is being a bully. Pushing, hitting, name-calling, and teasing are not OK. No one has the right to hurt you. Stand up for yourself and others. When have YOU said "**NO**"?

O **is for OPTIMISM**. Optimism is feeling hopeful that GOOD things will happen. Being optimistic is saying to yourself, "I Can Do This!" Positive thinking leads to positive results. If you feel frustrated, take a break. Can you break a task down into smaller steps to solve the problem? For example, learning how to ride a bike doesn't happen all at once. Being optimistic will empower you to solve a problem. Think positive, stay calm, and don't give up! How can **optimism** help YOU the next time you face a challenge?

P **is for PATIENCE.** Patience is wanting something without getting upset, complaining or giving up. Learning to be patient with others and yourself is part of life. Practicing patience can be so HARD, not everything happens as quickly as you want! Do you politely wait your turn to speak? Have you had to wait in a line or go on a long car ride? Planting a garden, mastering somersaults, or learning to play music takes time and patience. Take a deep breath and keep trying. You are capable and your effort will be worth it! When will YOU need **patience**?

Q is for **QUIET**. Everyone needs quiet time. It's not healthy for your mind or body to be BUSY all the time! Take breaks from your T.V., phone, and video games. Enjoying silence is as necessary as the air you breathe. Did you know that quiet time builds new cells in your brain for learning and memory, lowers stress, and promotes creativity? So, S-L-O-W down and connect to nature, daydream, or take a nap. When you Rest-Reset-Recharge you will feel calm and full of new energy! How often do YOU get **quiet** time?

R **is for RESPECT**. Showing respect means using good manners and treating people with equality, courtesy, and kindness. Self-respect is loving and valuing yourself-exactly as you are! Feeling pride and confidence in yourself leads to making good choices: like taking care of your body, watching your language, and behaving respectfully. You deserve to be treated with dignity and respect-as you should treat others the same. Who do YOU **respect** and why?

S is for **SERVICE**. Service to others means helping and expecting nothing in return. Donating pet food to an animal shelter, cleaning up litter in a park, or singing carols at a nursing home are examples of service. By doing one act of service, your kindness will spread outward like ripples in the water. Your good deed may affect others in ways you may never see. Be a good citizen and encourage your friends to volunteer. Your actions will inspire others to make a difference too. How have YOU **served** others?

T **is for TRUTH**. Telling the truth builds trust so others know they can believe you and count on you. Lying and making up things about people will make others mistrust you. Tell the truth, it is easier to remember! Being honest gives you peace. Be honest about mistakes you've made or accidents that happen. Speaking the truth takes courage. Be courageous, honest, and always tell the truth. Share a time when YOU were **truthful**.

U is for **UNIQUE**. As human beings, we are ALL Unique. You are as individual as a fingerprint, no two are the same. No one else has had the exact experiences or sees the world the way you do. There is only one you! Be happy with and LOVE who you are. Value your strengths; don't compare yourself to others. Your personality, your dreams, fears, talents and creativity are all unique to you! Celebrate diversity and the uniqueness of others. What a boring world it would be if we were all the exactly the SAME! You are amazing just by being you! What makes YOU **unique**?

V **is for VALUE.** To value something or someone means it is VERY important to you. Nature, animals, our planet, and time are valuable to us, but people are the most valued of all. We are different in age, color, beliefs, health, personality, and appearance, but full of unlimited potential. APPRECIATE, CHERISH, LOVE, RESPECT, and TREASURE are all words that express value. If you appreciate your friends, you value them. Loving your family means you value them. Do you have a pet you cherish? Value yourself, the differences of others, and respect ALL living things. Who or what is **valuable** to YOU?

W **is for WORLD.** We all live together in this BIG, beautiful world. Be a good citizen of the Earth and do your part to protect our water, air, and wildlife. REDUCE-REUSE-RECYCLE! Plastic bottles take 450 years to decompose, Aluminum cans 200 years, and plastic bags up to 1,000 years! OH MY! Did you know you can recycle paper, cardboard, glass, plastic, metal, tires, batteries and electronics? Planting trees cleans the air we breathe. Riding buses, bikes, or sharing rides saves energy. We MUST do our part to protect our wonderful planet Earth! How can YOU help our **world**?

X **is for eXpression**. Self-eXpression means expressing your personality, feelings, ideas, and opinions. Spark your creative self through art, music, dance, writing, or inventing. Creativity helps you reduce stress, promotes thinking, problem-solving skills, and puts you in a happy-creative zone. Writing a story, playing an instrument, painting, inventing, cooking, and being on stage are just a few ways to be eXpressive. You never know what masterpiece you may create. So, explore and uncover something new inside you! What are ways YOU **express** yourself?

Y **is for YOU**. You are like a puzzle. Your pieces are made from your own experiences. Your personality and knowledge shape your view of the world. Set goals, study hard, eat well, exercise, and be optimistic. Develop hobbies and strive to grow in your knowledge and independence a little more each day. Writing about your goals can help to guide and motivate you. We are all unique individuals and have talents to contribute. You have a purpose and mission in life. What makes you, **YOU**?

Z **is for ZEST**. Zest means living life with excitement and energy. Do you wake up in the morning excited and enthusiastic for what the day will bring? Are you curious and eager to learn new things? Live in the present moment and focus on what is around you. Use your senses to experience life's moments HERE and NOW! Each day you get to wake up to new opportunities: chances to learn, grow, and show gratitude. That is exciting! What makes YOU feel full of **zest**?

<u>YOU</u>

You Be YOU.

Let your inner light shine through.

You Be YOU.

Grow, learn and try something new.

You Be YOU.

Make this world a better place.

You Be YOU.

Put a smile on Someone's Face.

You Be YOU.

Laugh, create and do good deeds.

You Be YOU.

Be Aware of Other's Needs.

You Be YOU.

Respect your body and your health.

You Be YOU.

Stand up for others and yourself.

You Be YOU.

Display courage in all you do.

And Always remember—

YOU BE YOU!

by Mitzi Adams © 2020 Mitzi Adams Studio, LLC

What are YOUR goals? Take time to imagine YOUR future. What would YOU like to accomplish? Make a copy of this page and draw YOUR ideas inside the bubble clouds above.

How do you see yourself? Make a copy of this page and draw a self-portrait in the mirror. Think of words that best describe YOU and write them around the mirror. Color and cut out to make a bookmark and remember: "You are Amazing just by being YOU!"

ABOUT THE AUTHOR

Mitzi Adams, M.Ed, is a former Elementary teacher. In addition to teaching and raising her family, she has worked as a private tutor, bookkeeper, and community volunteer.

Her advocacy for women and children includes literacy tutoring and the role of chairperson and board member for various community, school, and fundraising events. Featured in the 2017 Keeneland magazine for her non-profit volunteer work, Mitzi has merged her inner artist, teaching, and life experiences as inspiration for her first book.

A-Z For Me! Life Skills for Kids was written to facilitate dialogue with parents, teachers, and children. It is her hope to encourage the strengths of all children, expand their empathy, empower them through challenges, and to equip them for success.

Mitzi resides in Nicholasville, Kentucky with her husband and has three adult children. She can be found writing, quilting, and making art with her three fur babies by her side. Visit mitziadamsstudio.com for her latest art endeavors, blogs, Children's Book Anthology and Parent Resources. You can also connect on Facebook and Instagram @mitziadamsstudio or mitziadamsstudio@gmail.com.

ABOUT THE ILLUSTRATOR

Lindsey Jaeger is an award-winning fine artist, illustrator, practicing patent attorney, wife, mother, homeschool teacher of daughters, Lily and Iris, and founder of Creativity Sparkler.

Inspiration for the illustrations found in this book came from Lindsey's own childhood spent playing in her treehouse, rolling down hills, swinging on swings her dad made her, and painting. On any given Saturday, you may find Lindsey climbing a barge rope or up a tree with her daughters on her parents' farm in Kentucky.

To purchase originals or prints of her nature art or to commission her to illustrate your next book, learn more at lindseyjaeger.com. Connect on Facebook and Instagram @LindseyJaegerFineArt.

As founder of Creativity Sparkler, Lindsey provides emerging artists and authors inspiration via weekly emails and podcast episodes, and one-on-one coaching to overcome obstacles on the way to achieving creative goals. Learn more at creativitysparkler.com. Connect on Facebook and Instagram @CreativitySparkler.